Running with Daffodils

Samantha R.S.

ISBN: 9798677260919

"Why are you smiling in the face of death," asked the Marigold.

"Because it will invite a hundred more births," replied the Daffodil.

DEDICATION

For my mother and father,
You gave me words to hold me
in the times when you could not.

For Ryan,
You have pulled the beast from my bones
and made me soft again.

Daffodils must die

You must have misunderstood

When I said that
I wanted you to be my sun,
I meant that I desired
For my body to be warmed
And my skin kissed
By your very existence,
And not that I wanted to be
So burnt by your presence
That I couldn't recognize
Who I was anymore.

Breaking

It is not your leaving,
But the way you left
That breaks me
Continuously.

Blood

You need to know that
It isn't only lovers who are
Capable of breaking your spine
With the weight of
Unrequitedness.
That, sometimes, it is the blood
That drenches you in more hurt
Than the water.

Trampled

You walked in
And you didn't take your shoes off.
It was as though you knew
You had no intentions of staying.
And through my home,
You trampled,
Before walking out again.

I keep leaving the door open.

Log kya kehenge?
What will people say?

"Believe in God," they said.
So, I did, and they stoned me
For believing in the wrong one.

"Respect your elders," they said.
So, I did, and they cursed me
For wanting respect in return.

"Worship your husband," they said.
So, I did, and they spat on me
For sitting on the shrine beside him.

"Cover your body," they said.
So, I did, and they still plunged
Their fingers into my chastity.

Resentment

It feels like the thorns
Of a thousand roses
Driving through the palms
Of these hands that prayed for you,
Painfully.
How I resent the way
I still look for you.
Waiting for you to love me
Is like planting a flower in concrete
And waiting for it to bloom.

Hungry

This body
Sprouts love
Like the natural resource
That keeps on giving,
And sits at the mercy
Of hungry hands
That keep on taking.

Buried

I swallowed the key
To the coffin.
When you are away,
I go to visit
That piece of me
That you asked I bury
In the name of love.
And when we part,
She begs that I leave
A crack in the door
Because she longs
To keep breathing.

Ugly

It was only after
The flowers wilted
And lovers lost their chance
At Summer romancing,
Had the sun realized that
Quieting her flame to become
A lukewarm version of beautiful
Was the ugliest thing she could do.

Souvenirs

These bones
Will forever carry
The stories that you have branded
Onto them.
Souvenirs from that time
You came,
You vacationed.

Second Chance

If a rose
Wrapped in cellophane
Could talk,
I imagine she would ask
For a second chance –
Not only to be held
Like a dying accessory
In the hands of her lover,
But to be rooted in his garden
Among all the other things
That deserve to live.

Hourglass

I will sit by the window
And count every grain of sand
That passes through the hourglass,
Begrudgingly,
As I wait for you
To show me that you love me.
To show me how to love me.

Expired

Cognac swirls
Around the curves of my tongue,
Between the pulls of nicotine
That hit the back of my throat.
I tease my palate
With soft drags of the blade.

Anything
To rid myself
Of the bitter taste
Of your expired love.

Blood

My heart spills
Onto the ground
Where you walk.
You will forever carry
The blood of my suffering
Beneath your feet.

Leaving

There were times when
I would wish death
On you.
Not because I wanted it,
But because the idea
Of you
Leaving a whole world
Was easier to swallow
Than the idea
Of you
Leaving me.

Home

How do you expect
Your beautiful flesh
To feel like home
When you insist
On booking it
Like a bed and breakfast?

Inside

I pity the man
Who can only see
The outside of that woman –
The way her tresses fall
Along the curves of her backside,
And her sugary West Indian skin.
So stunted is his vision
That he cannot see
The place she's made for him
Inside of her.

God

For your sake,
I tried to get to know God,
So that I could pray
Your lust for me
Into love.

I am convinced now
That He is imaginary.

Coward

Haunting thoughts of you
Crawl onto my body
And dig their way in
Under my skin.
In the thick of the night,
I bleed,
And the coward inside me
Begs that I let you in.

You can put love
In a radioactive bottle
And we will still drink from it,
Euphorically.

Greedy

He was greedy
For all the love
That I had, contained,
In this frail body,
So I gave it all to him
And kept none for myself.
How could I be
So selfless
And selfish
At once?

Vicariously

I remember being his flower –
Sitting out on the cobbled stoop
Where he left me,
My happiness at the mercy of the sun,
Until I withered, and fell apart,
My scorched petals brushing against
The dust of the ground.
He piled my death into his palms
And put them in the bind
Of a romance novel,
With sullen eyes,
To live vicariously through its words.
He cared for them fervently.
He cared for them
A little too late.

Heart

I wish you hadn't
Grown so fickle –
Breaking yourself into
A thousand pieces
As he leaves.
Heaving yourself
Back into place
As he returns.

When will you learn?

Some have bled
For the freedom
That I walk on.

Some will bleed
For the freedom
Of those after me.

There is nothing free about it.

-      *for those who have fought.*

Vacant

Too many times
Have I kicked self-love
Out the door,
Like the unpaying tenant,
To make myself vacant
For you.

I only have me to blame.

Karma

In the times
When I wish
To destroy you,
Like you, me,
I remind myself that
You have already
Signed that contract
With your karma.

Promises

I cannot imagine
What the sunflower must feel.
She, who is so in love
That she has taken his name,
Waits for him to kiss her awake
And spends her days
Dancing for him.
And only with the promise
Of tomorrow,
He leaves his flower
To woo another.

And, she waits.

Debt

His was
A borrowed kind
Of intimacy.
So tall had
My overdues piled
That I sold
A piece of myself
To pay for it.

Duty

The women's voices crack when
They talk about their husbands.
Her soft heart wants so desperately
To believe that he is a good man.
So much so that she makes him
Talkari with a side of excuses
For dinner.
She pulls the words from behind
Her teeth to make conversation,
Hoping today was not like yesterday.
Her plastic-clad troubles go out with
The trash because there is simply
No room in this house for it.
He occupies all the space in here,
And that is that.
How could they try to convince me
That this is the way to love?
Love and subservience are not
Cut from the same cloth.

Purgatory

Some lovers were not meant
To be a forever after.
Some were only meant
To be the purgatory
That prepares you for
The paradise after her.

Foolish

Foolish honeybee,
Can't you see?
That darling marigold
Is only a mirage.
There is no nectar
Waiting for you.

Foolish honeybee.
Foolish me.

Bloom

How does it feel
To be
Inside of that woman
Searching for roses
That would not bloom?

Casual

My insides brim
With all the questions
I could not ask,
like
how do you turn
carnal nights
into casual goodbyes
so easily,
so quickly?
I have never been able
To greet the tide
Without wanting the ocean,
Like you.

Triumph

Death and triumph
Share a bed.
It is only after
Some lovers reunite
At the gates
Of promised land,
Can their love prevail.

Searching

We invited each other
To the wild –
Our writhing bodies
And searching hands
Trying to pull the beasts
From our bones,
Trying to find softness
Under bosoms of stone.

Burial

I am not required to be
The flesh that you
Dig graves into
To hide all the things that
You are trying to run away from,
Only to sprout weeds that
You won't even tend to.
I am nobody's burial ground.

Expiration

This stomach
Aches of you.
My limbs are weak
And quivering,
And my tongue –
Dry and deprived.
It would seem that
I consumed a love
That has turned
Sour.

Thirst

I look at my mother and father
Tend to their garden –
The gentleness of limbs that
Care for the flowers,
And the overflowing nectar pots
So hummingbirds know no thirst.

My five-year-old self longs
To have been a garden.

Melting

I was foolish to think
That I could find heaven
In you.
I should have known when
I found myself
Walking through your fire,
The sugar melting off my skin.

Mortal

And if you ever feel
Like your ego has grown
Too big for your body,
Call out to me
And let me remind you
Of the mortal beneath the shrine.

Sin

You crawled your way
Into me
Like sin to Eden.
How long were you
Expecting this
Paradise to last?

To be born again

Petrichor

And just when I thought that
My dying body was ready
To be turned into ashes
And lowered into forgottenness,
The rains poured down
With such arousal that
Even the Gods could smell
The life returning
To my once parched limbs.

Be mine.

From me, to me.

Drunk

If you ever sipped
From the parts of you
That have left me
Drunk and foolish,
Even you would
Start believing
In the Gods
And their alchemy.

Wither

All of the ego
That sat on my chest –
She withered,
She died,
On the day
My father cried.

Sunkissed

Be her sun –
The only thing that could
Kiss her skin,
Prying her out of slumber,
That could weave gold
Through her hair
And bury warmth
Beneath her pores
To keep her remembering you
Until you see her again
Tomorrow.

Home

I will strip myself down
To my very core –
To the parts of me where
The light of the sun
Makes love to the moon
And the auroras romance
With the darkness
To show you that,
Much like this Universe,
I am your home.

Unchanged

Having born the weight
Of you and your brothers,
The Universe has taken you
Into the palm of her hands
And has pleaded
With your purgatory.
Until her knees are calloused
And her well runs dry,
She petitions for your sake.

I cannot imagine the tragedy if,
After all of this,
You emerged unsoftened,
Unchanged.

Full

Be
A human so full
That you meet
Graveyard violets
With the same rapture
As velvet roses.

Gypsy

My nights
Are more alive
Than my mornings.
It is only when
Darkness falls
And the smell
Of evening jasmine
Perfumes the air
That thoughts of you
Gypsy through my body.

Worth

How lucky are we
To be romanced by the sun
And guarded by the moon,
To be loved by the day
And protected by the night?
What more can we ask for
From this Universe
Who set our worth
Among her stars?

Soft

I was born with
A heart so soft
That my bones refused
To carry the weight
Of the responsibility
Of her safe keeping.

I was born with my heart
In my hands.

Summer's Rain

It is the space between
Your chest and mine
That doubt comes to die,
That the thunderstorm
Greets the sunshine
And is boiled down
To a Summer's Rain.

When I lay with you.

Home

Sweet brown girl,
This body is home.
Her door is not revolving.
You let her visitors know
That they knock
Before entering
And take their shoes off.
Even flowers find refuge
In her dusky skin
When they have grown
Too tall and too far
From the soil.

Sweet brown girl,
Before you furnish rooms
And set tables
For anyone else,
Make yourself at home.

Seduce

Love and nature
Share the law
Of seduction.

It is only
When you learn
To seduce the thorns,
That they let you
Romance their roses.

Father

It would be remiss of me to disregard your
Suffering, and the sacrifices you have carried
On your back for so long. They are loudest
During the silence between the few words and
Phrases we exchange – when we both grapple for
The next leading topic of discussion. I spent many
Nights hoping I wouldn't turn out like you – that
Your anger and anxiety were not as hereditary as
Your eyes. Look at me now. It was as though my
Maker grew tired and used your blueprint as a
Cheat sheet to my becoming. And, now that I am
You, I cannot help but wonder if the same things
That are breaking me have already broken you.
If your limbs have grown tired of the same fight
That I have only just begun. Though you try to
Mend in silence, you do not mend alone.
Father, I see you.

Selflessness

I want to remind you
Of her selflessness –
That everything she has given to herself,
She gave to you first.
She buried the stars beneath your eyes
Before scattering them across her own body,
And bosomed the conviction of the sun
Before furnishing the horizon,
And the parts of you that she left in darkness
Were made to canvas
The lights of your soul.

Bone Deep

Her love
Runs bone deep
Through him,
Dressing fractures
Once caused by
The weight
Of mourning.

Home

One day,
You will find yourself
Knocking on
Your own door.
When you do,
Let you in
And make yourself
A home.

Identity

I wipe the day off my face,
Only to unearth yours –
Eyes, beautiful and tired,
Laugh lines that only deepen with time,
And bronzed cheek bones,
A canvas for the tears
Of your struggles.
No matter how hard I try to find
My own identity in this world,
I will always be left
With ripples of you
In a sea of me.

-    *For my mother and father*

Frolic

I love the way
The wind frolics
With the flames –
Just enough turbulence
To send it wild,
But gentle enough
To keep it ablaze.

I am your flame
On windy days.

With You

I want to ask time
To pause and hasten
All at once, because
I want to sink into
This feeling of our now,
But discover all the things
Buried in my tomorrow
With you.

Regrets

I have kissed the lips
Of death before,
And for it,
I have no regrets.
It is because of this
Estranged affair
That I can make love
To life.

We

Threads of your chestnut hair
Weave through the woolen carpet
In all the places we spilled our love.
And when I look in the mirror,
I see you looking back at me,
Because we've spent so much time
With lips locked and barely
A crack between our chests
For our cosmos to breathe,
That I became you,
That you became me.

On Healing

Nothing can prepare you for the labor that
Comes with healing. Trauma, like an axe
Dug into the bark of an oak tree, requires
You to exhaust yourself in the name of its
Undoing. Your wounds will need to itch,
And tighten, and scab over.
Your nights will be agonizing,
As you sleep on the things that
You are trying to repair.
You will realize that you are travelling
A one-way street that won't allow you
To turn around.
I cannot tell you that healing is easy,
But it is the only thing that can do what no
Beloved, or shaman, or antidote can.
It is the only thing that
Can save you.

Collapsing

And in the end,
The stars were all
That were left
In the company
Of an aching heart
To remind him that
Even they could not exist
Without first collapsing.

Primrose

The primrose
Gives herself up
To the night,
Letting go of
A sun who
Would not stay.

Letters

Sometimes,
I write letters to my afterlife,
Asking for my safekeeping.
I tell them how I like my coffee,
And the kind of fountain pens I prefer
To write with. I plead that, should I be
Given a second chance on Earth,
My fears are not wasted on things as
Frivolous as butterflies and the dark.
I make a list of the things I wish to keep
And the things I wish to erase.
When I write a letter to my afterlife,
I write it twice.
I post one to heaven and one to hell.
I want to make sure I have covered
All my bases.

Foreplay

It is easy
To make you want me
For my body.
But to have you
Lust my mind –
That is the only challenge
I am willing to accept.

Easy is not
My foreplay of choice.

Better Half

You have spent too many nights
Searching for completeness
In a world that has always
Made you feel incomplete,
To only be deemed as
My better half.
I will tell stories to the flowers
About how you,
My love,
Are my better whole.

Man and God

Everyone talks about the Gods like they want
To someday be one. Like, if they spoke long and
Reverent enough, life after death will meet them
In the heavens upon a shrine. So, I question
Mortality and immortality, only set apart by the
Unit of time.

I wonder what it must be like to live each day
Knowing that your existence is infinite. Is there
Even the slightest thirst for living and loving and
Breathing? Do you feign the desire to live
Every day like it would be your last?

Give me my mortality. Let me lose myself in
The thrill of running along the timeline of life,
And let me find peace in my very last breath.

Again

I let the sun
Weave his warmth
Through my undressed limbs
And keep my blood
Running hot
Until I could
Have you again.

Emptiness

These words
Have moved through me
In the times when
I wanted to feel nothing at all.
They marched into the room,
Like a jealous lover,
To pull me from the bed
Where I romanced
With the emptiness,
To reclaim their love.

Ego

I watched you wither away
And the nothingness polish you off.
As I stood there, in my canary dress,
I watched them wrap you in white cotton
And lower you into your forever after.

My darling,
Death looks good on you.

Conviction

You did not raise me
With a fire raging
Within the depths of my belly
To be okay with anything less
Than what was meant to be
For me.
I will set the world ablaze
With my conviction.

Unrequitedness

For it is unrequitedness
That has allowed me
To make peace with
My wanting
To love and to feel
On my own terms
In a space where
There is only enough
For one of us to receive.

Twilight

His
Is a love
That brought
The twilight
To her knees,
For she was
No longer
The most beautiful
Thing in the room.

Dusk knows no narcissist
Greater than the sun.

She is his most
Self-absorbed hour.

Jannah

You have been
My Jannah
On this Earth,
In this life.

-   *grandmother*

Deserving

To say that I am not
Deserving of love
Is to say that the trees
Are not deserving of the rain
Or the stars
Of the sun.
I would never wish for you
To be deprived of the things
That breathe life into you.
Then why, in God's name,
Would I wish that for me?

Quenched

The shore –
Her thirst can
Never be quenched
By trickles of water
Cascading off her body.
She longs to be consumed
By an entire ocean,
Over and over again.

Designer

Whether love is
Enough or not
Depends on your
Brand of it.

Chaos

I didn't think
There could be
A softer,
Gentler way
To say my name
Until it rolled off your lips
And quelled the chaos
Inside of me.

Outgrown

Like the tattered shoe
That could no longer cushion
A tired sole.
Like the taste of milk
That the palate
Once-upon-a-time craved.
Like the pot
That can no longer
Hold the plant whose roots
Long to stretch into
The belly of the Earth,
People outgrow people.

Undress

When a woman
Undresses her thoughts –
Strips them bare
And lays them before you,
Desire them,
Devour them.

Her body can wait.

Alive

Feel
Your zealous heart
Lay into
The woolen mattress.
In times of lifelessness,
Let it remind you
That you are alive.

On Pain

When I was a little girl, I walked in on my mother.
She was curled up in the corner of her bed,
Pain-ridden. Fear spilled through every cell in
My body and sat on my chest, for my brain had
Only learned to associate pain with anguish.

She called me in and sat me on her, nestled in
Her bosom. This was the day that I learned that
Not all pain come from dark places. That,
Sometimes, it can flow from places of light and
Hope – like a woman's miraculous ability to bear
Life onto the Earth, who will trace in her footsteps
Until he can stamp footprints of his own.

To my mother and the generations of women
Before her, I dedicate the fruits of my suffering.

Judgement Day

I want to be
So sure of myself that
The Gods and Demons
Stand at the gates
And watch me choose
My own fate,
When judgement day comes.

A Reason

It is the very dirt
On the surface of this Earth
That gives me a reason to live –
That she is walked on,
Trampled,
Dug up and spaded,
Yet, somehow,
Bears life to some of the most
Beautiful flowers.
And when I sink my toes
Into her dusky body,
I can feel my resolve growing.
I can feel my inner-most
Beauty birthing.

Burdens

Tell my daughter
That my back was strong –
Enough to carry the burdens
Of my mother,
And her mother,
And hers.
Tell her that I grew gardens
With their tears
And bore new life
From their blood.

Tell my daughter
I did this for her.

Walls

How ironic
Is it that
We construct
Impenetrable walls
To guard us from
The outside,
Only to be enclosed
With the demons
Living inside.

Let them greet
Each other
With ferity.

Cascade

I have never resented
A warm shower
As much as the one
That washes the smell of you
Off of me.
I watch your magic
Cascade off my skin
And down the drain,
Only to do it all over again.

Wilderness

I was born with the wilderness
Brewing in my chest.
How else do I explain
This thirst
To run with the wolves,
Feet bare,
And roam my father's Earth
Without fear?

Peace

Peace is not
The absence of the storm.
Peace is
The home that is built
Upon the rocks,
When the tempest is
Most wrathful,
With bricks and shutters
Made for safekeeping.
Peace is
Realizing that you
Are the home
That will brave the storm.

Sati

Don't you walk through fire
For the one
Whose love for you
Has turned to ash
And gone with the tide.
You will only be losing yourself.

Prerogative

"Why do you write?" they asked.

"Why do you breathe?" I replied.

This is my imperative.
When my feelings well up
And translate to thoughts
That flood the insides of me,
Like the very breath that
Fills your lungs,
Like an internal hemorrhage,
I need to save myself.
So, on paper,
I bleed.

"But what if you become forgotten?"
chimed the Aster.

"The sun will keep you remembering
me."

Thank You

For being present. For reading mindfully. For feeling, unapologetically, until the very last page, I thank you.

When I began my poetry writing journey, I did not think that it would bring me here – with a book in hand and a circle of people who believed in it. You can probably tell, by now, that I am one who loves boundlessly, cracks easily, and heals tenderly. If not with my words, how else do I make sense of this storm inside of me? Thank you for sharing in that.

I have nothing but gratitude in my heart, upon reaching this point – for the people who played an active role in my writing and publishing process, and for those who have led me to feeling so intensely, giving birth to a melee of emotions and, of course, these poems. Most importantly, I thank those who stand around me today, cheering me on. You, having read this book, are one of them.

Samantha R.S.

About the Author

Nestled within the murky Gulf of Paria, the turbulent North Atlantic, and the beautiful Caribbean Ocean lies the dual islands of Trinidad and Tobago. A diverse country whose culture and history embrace layers of struggle, pain, triumph, and joy. From this rich blend of experiences was born Samantha R.S. - friend, woman, educator, artist, and author - clinging to tradition and forging personal rebellion, ultimately choosing expression over suppression. Samantha is an old soul who views life with sensitivity, sincerity, wit, and a dash of sarcasm. Her days are filled with teaching, music, fitness, travel, crafting, and coffee. Above all, in her heart of hearts, she is happiest when creating and expressing. Samantha is heart deep into a long and beautiful love affair with words. Within them lies the comfort of an old friend, the hope of a sunrise, the passion of a lover, and the healing of a shaman. Through them, she purges the pain of the moment, liberates the shackles of the past, and transcends the obstacles of the moment. This process expels demons while giving birth to hope, mending wounds, and healing souls. Through the alchemy of empathy, Samantha refines emotions, transforming them into precious images of the mind's eye. With blood, sweat, and tears, her life experiences morph into feelings and then her feelings into words. With those words, she paints emotional portraits, baring her naked heart and soul. Both hauntingly dark and hopefully bright she captures the emotional ups and downs of the human condition. Samantha's connection from earth to stars is gripping, vivid and relatable, inviting the reader into her soul while transporting them to a resonating memory, fear, or dream of their own experience.

Samantha R.S. has the courage to embrace the darkness, searching deep within the abyss for the glimmer of light growing within us all. She guides us, finding the beauty and contradiction, the harmony within the chaos, and the hope resurrected from despair. Enjoy this journey out of the darkness into the light. Samantha reminds readers that even in the darkest of times we can stoke the inner glow of a better tomorrow, and through this we can feel, and we will heal.

John Steinbach

Connect with Me

Join me on this bewitching journey.
Grow with me, feel with me, write with me.
Find me on Instagram
r.s.samantha

The daffodil flower is a symbol of rebirth. She blooms
for only a part of the year and dies when her time is up.
It is in the period between wilting and blossoming that
the flower reaches within herself to rejuvenate and
repair, in preparation for her next moment of birth.

Running with Daffodils is a collection of poems about
the dying – the hurting, the defeat; and the rebirth – the
healing, the triumph.

* 9 7 9 8 6 7 7 2 6 0 9 1 9 *